CROSSING
A NARROW BRIDGE

CROSSING
A NARROW BRIDGE

CONNOR TIFARRA

For Theresa and Sasha

CONTENTS

Alone She Cries   1

So Lovely Is She   4

Such A Beautiful Girl   6

Love Is What She Wants   8

I Tripped and Fell In Love   10

We're In Love with Each Other   12

Key To My Heart   15

Two Young Lovers   17

Let's Fly Away   19

Straight To Your Heart   21

Rainy Day Girl   24

She's a Country Lady   26

I Dreamed I Was You   28

The Brave   31
Back To Back   33
Broken Promises   37
Nothing Lasts   40
21 Lovers Lane   42
Letting Go of Love   44
Sometimes You Win, Sometimes You Lose   46
It's Been a Good Life   48
Next Time You're Lonely   50
Watching the Wagon Wheel Roll 'Round   52
Roses, Rainbows and You   54
Looking At the Outside   56
Holly   58
Time Plays the Game   60
Trapped   62
Turn My Life Around   65
Delusions   67
I'm Feeling Down   69
I'll Have to Dream Alone   71
The Decision   74
Love Should Come Easy   77
A Letter Left Behind   79
San Francisco Dreams   81
Billy's First Baseball Game   83
Bare Bones   87
The Widowed Wife   89
Tunnel Runner   90

I Have Had It All   92
Another Lost Soul   93
Illusions Within   94
Infliction   95
The End Is Closer Than the Beginning   96
I Am Just a Man   97
34 Years Gone   99
Open Wounds   100
Forever Friends   101
Can You Feel Me?   102
Precious Life   103
Reaching Out   104
Silent Screams   105
A Different Way   107
I Walk On Thorns   109
Starting Over   111
The Colors of My World   112
With Open Arms   114

CROSSING
A NARROW BRIDGE

ALONE SHE CRIES

Alone she cries
Hoping her pain will go away
She's disappointed in herself
Her world is in dismay

Voices echo in her mind
From the memories of her past
Her dreams are only nightmares
How long will they last?

The fruit of life falls from the trees
Her failures and misfortunes bring her to her knees
She knows there is no one else to blame
She hides in the corner
She hangs her head in shame

She puts herself on trial
Being her own judge and jury
Sentencing herself to life in her inner prison
She walks the floor inside her box wanting to scream
Though she has no mouth

She fights her own loneliness
Not wanting to live and yet...
So afraid to die

Alone she cries

Perhaps as the years painfully pass
She will discover new portals in her box
Gateways that shall take her to new worlds
Life of freedom
No chains
No locks

What will it take to make her escape?
How much suffering must she endure?
Perhaps the time will come
With another turn of the sun
Will she find happiness once more?

She dreams of her handsome Prince Charming
Arriving on a chariot with wings
Sweeping her away from the lonesome valley
Showing her beautiful things
But the chariot's wings are broken
She will never see her claim to fame
Her Prince disappears in the midst
Her eyes cry like the rain

A steady stream flows from her face to her feet
Out of her room, through her house and into the street
Through canyons and valleys
Through towns and alleys
Into lakes and seas
Becoming a part of you...
Living inside of me

Alone she cries

She travels on a river of betrayal
Hands reach out from the water removing her veil
She tempts the raging rapids
Challenging her own fears
Sunshine touches her eyes
Above her are endless skies
Will she reach the shore and be saved from undeserved
sorrow?

Her existence is spared before the waterfall
Now she stands tall
Breaking down the walls that separated her from the living
No more falls
Taking each step with a brand new meaning
Believing
Crossing a narrow bridge with strength and courage
Celebrating a new beginning

She knows there's hope for tomorrow
Now that she's living for today
Released from her past
She's free at last
Realizing she was never alone at all

SO LOVELY IS SHE

So lovely is she
In the morning sun
Waking to a new day
Her life has just begun

She chases the rainbows of her far away dreams
In a field of daisies and crystal clear streams
The fragrance of pomegranates scent the air
Camphire leaves decorate her hair

So lovely is she
In the mid-day rain
Feeding from the tree of paradise
Harvesting the grain

She dances in the valley
Where the mountain ash colors the sands
Pools created from the rains
Give new life across the land

So lovely is she
As the sun departs the sky
Her smile brightens the darkness
The Moon reflects in her eyes

She lays down in a meadow of frankincense trees
Sleeping through the night
Creating new dreams

That's where she finds
In the depths of her mind
A world the way she wishes it could be

A world made of happiness and love
Her beauty is love
So lovely is she

SUCH A BEAUTIFUL GIRL

I went out late last night
Hoping to catch the sight of a beautiful girl
I went to my favorite club called Little White Dove
Just down the hill

When I walked into the room I could smell her perfume
She was sitting at a table all alone, I couldn't help but stare
I looked into her eyes then she took me by surprise
When she waived come over here

Then she took me by the hand
Straight to the dance floor we ran

We danced all night long while the band played her favorite
love songs
We laughed and talked
How we carried on
I was lucky last night
To catch the sight of a beautiful girl
Such a beautiful girl

Her hair smelled like roses
When I held her close and we danced cheek to cheek
Her eyes were hypnotizing, her lips were so inviting
That I could hardly speak

Then she put her lips to mine
I almost lost my mind

We danced all night long while the band played her favorite
love songs
We laughed and talked
How we carried on
I was lucky last night
To catch the sight of a beautiful girl
Such a beautiful girl

I wonder if I'm ever going to see her again
Or smell her perfume in the summer wind
I can't pretend
She was out of this world
She was such a beautiful girl

I was lucky last night
I caught the sight of a beautiful girl
Such a beautiful girl
She was such a beautiful girl

LOVE IS WHAT SHE WANTS

This girl's all alone
She doesn't want it that way
She'd love to settle down and have a family someday
She's always wanted someone
To treat her like a queen
So far, that's still a dream

Loneliness can hurt
Life can seem so tough
When there's no one to love you
And you want to be loved
Dreams can fall apart
Just as fast as they came
She doesn't understand it
She's not to blame

All she wants is to be in love
She's been alone for long enough
Reaching a dream can seem so tough
But she's never giving up

Love is what she wants
Love is what she needs
Love will win her heart
Love is what it takes
Love is what she wants
Love is what she needs
If you want to know this girl

Give her all the love that she needs

She has a heart of gold
She's not too bold
She's a little shy until she meets the right guy
She loves to sing and dance
She really wants the chance
To show someone who she is inside

But her dreams still linger on
This girl is still all alone
How long will this go on?
She hopes it not too long
With this girl you can't go wrong
Love is what she wants

She's always dreamed of being in love
She's been alone for long enough
Reaching a dream can seem so tough
But she's never giving up

Love is what she wants
Love is what she needs
Love will win her heart
Love is what it takes
Love is what she wants
Love is what she needs
If you want to know this girl
Give her all the love that she needs

I TRIPPED
AND FELL IN LOVE

I was in the right place at just the right time
To see you walking by
When you least expect it to come your way
Loves finds its way to you

I don't know how I passed you by
I must have been looking at the sky
This fast paced world almost led me astray
Until I met you on the corner that day

The timing was right
To see each other in the sunlight
It was love at first sight
When I saw her eyes shine brightly
She smiled and said hello
Ever since that day I've loved her so

Love can sneak up on you
It's a crazy thing
Somehow love found you
And brought you all the way to me

I don't know how love does it
I only know I love it
I never thought I'd fall in love
But I tripped and fell in love that day

I use to fall too hard and love passed me up
This time I stumbled
But I had good luck
Now she loves me and my pick-up truck
I tripped and fell in love

The timing was right
To see each other in the sunlight
It was love at first sight
When I saw her eyes shine brightly
She smiled and said hello
Ever since that day I've loved her so

Love can sneak up on you
It's a crazy thing
Somehow love found you
And brought you all the way to me

I don't know how love does it
I only know I love it
I never thought I'd fall in love
But I tripped and fell in love that day

I use to fall too hard and love passed me up
This time I stumbled
But I had good luck
Now she loves me and my pick-up truck
I tripped and fell in love

WE'RE IN LOVE
WITH EACH OTHER

She's something special
She's everything I need
She makes life blissful
From front to back and in between

Every time she kisses me
I feel the beating of my heart
When she's lying next to me
I know what we are

We're in love with each other
I'm just right for her
She's perfect for me
We're in love with each other
We fit together perfectly
We're so happy
Our love comes naturally
I love her and she loves me

She loves the moonlight
And root beer floats on a rainy night
She makes me thankful
She fills my heart with delight

Every time she kisses me
I feel the beating of my heart

When she's lying next to me
I know what we are

We're in love with each other
I'm just right for her
She's perfect for me
We're in love with each other
We fit together perfectly
We're so happy
Our love comes naturally
I love her and she loves me

She knows I love her
I say it to her everyday
She's sweet like nectar
Like a hummingbird we fly away

Every time we kiss
We feel the beating of our hearts
When she's lying next to me
We both know what we are

We're in love with each other
I'm just right for her
She's perfect for me
We're in love with each other
We fit together perfectly
We so happy
Our love comes naturally

We're in love with each other
I'm just right for her

She's perfect for me
We're in love with each other
We fit together perfectly
We so happy
Our love comes naturally
I love her and she loves me

KEY TO MY HEART

You own the key to my heart
My love belongs to you
I knew it right from the start
When you unlocked my heart
That I would give it to you

I never felt like this
All it took was your kiss
You had my heart doing flips
I've been living in bliss
Since I fell in love

I've never felt a love this strong
I know it can't be wrong
My heart's been locked up inside me for so long
There's no need to hide it
I'm so excited
It's a love I never knew
I'm so in love with you

You own the key to my heart
My love belongs to you
I knew it right from the start
When you unlocked my heart
That I would give it to you

My heart's been broke a few times
That was enough for me

It's been torn all apart
I put a lock on my heart
And hid the key

It's one of a kind
It can't be replaced
You can't duplicate this key
There's only one of me
And one key to my heart

I've never felt a love this strong
I know it can't be wrong
My heart chose you to love all my life long
There's no need to hide it
I'm so excited
It's a love that's all brand new
I'm so in love with you

You own the key to my heart
My love belongs to you
I knew it right from the start
When you unlocked my heart
That I would give it to you

I knew it right from the start
When you unlocked my heart
That I would give it to you

TWO YOUNG LOVERS

We are two young lovers
Loving each other
We'll always be together
Just you and me
No matter what they say
No one can break us away
Today, tomorrow and forever

I give you my heart
It's yours to keep
I'll always be yours for all eternity
I'll cherish you for all my life
And always be by your side

I'll sit at the top of the world with you
No one can tell us what we should do
We'll hold on to each other
No one can break through
Because no one can stop two young lovers
From loving each other

The worries of life will all fade away
Time is on our side
Don't be afraid
We'll find the strength we need
Love will be our guide

I hear some people say we're just too young

They don't really know us
They are so wrong
No matter what they say
They can't take us away
Today, tomorrow and forever

I'll sit at the top of the world with you
No one can tell us what we should do
We'll hold on to each other
No one can break through
Because no one can stop two young lovers
From loving each other

LET'S FLY AWAY

There's never been a love like ours on the planet Earth or in
the universe
I give you the heavens and the stars

You know I've never been to Mars
I've dreamed of traveling to the stars with you
Our love is true

Let's build a rocket and fly away
We'll live our life our own way
Don't be afraid
I'll show you the way

Let's fly away
Take my hand it will be ok
Let's fly away, fly away

Our love is new but meant to last
Forever we'll be, you don't have to ask
Eternity is on our side

We won't have to run and hide
Or keep our love locked deep inside
We'll be free, to do as we please

Let's build a rocket and fly away
We'll live our life our own way
Don't be afraid

I'll show you the way

Let's fly away
Take my hand it will be ok
Let's fly away, fly away

We'll always be together
It's you and me forever
Just like the world we were meant to be
We'll find a planet we can inhabit
Just you wait and see
Oh how I love you
Fly away with me

STRAIGHT TO YOUR HEART

It's hard on a soldier
When they have to go away
Defenders of freedom
Helping the world see a brighter day

Don't worry about me
I'm doing ok
I'll be home soon
I can't wait for that day

All my love is in every word I write
All my love is in my prayers each night
So don't be afraid
Don't cry a tear
I'll be home soon dear
Until then,

Straight to your heart
I'm sending my love
Straight to your heart
On the wings of a dove
And it won't be long
'Till I come home
I'm sending my love to your heart

Fighting for freedom
No one should have to do
Freedom should come easy

From my point of view

Some people live in the dark
They can't see any light
Instead of living a good life
We're watching people die

I don't know why the world has to be this way
I don't know why peace is so hard
But I'm not afraid
Don't cry a tear
I'll be home soon dear
Until then,

Straight to your heart
I'm sending my love
Straight to your heart
On the wings of a dove
And it won't be long
'Till I come home
I'm sending my love to your heart

I hope and pray
This war will be over soon
Then I'll be on a plane
Coming home to you

I'll hold you in my arms
I'll feel your touch again
Don't be afraid
No need for tears
I'll be home soon dear

Until then,

Straight to your heart
I'm sending my love
Straight to your heart
On the wings of a dove
And it won't be long
'Till I come home
I'm sending my love to your heart

No it won't be long
'Till I come home
I'm sending my love to your heart

RAINY DAY GIRL

You wandered around
When rainy days got you down
You thought the whole world was falling around you
I found you alone
No love of your own
No one to hold you when you're feeling lonely

I saw you so many times
When you'd walk by I knew I had to know you
Couldn't get you off my mind
That's when I knew that I just had to have you
To feel you
To make love to you

I could walk in the rain by your side
Then you wouldn't need the rain to hide the tears you cry
When rainy days get you down
I would always be around
Then you wouldn't be alone in this world
I'll be your rainy day girl

I didn't have the courage to say hello
The something deep inside me said don't let him go
This is my chance I better take it now
Or I'll never know just how I might have changed his world
I'll be his rainy day girl

Now you're my man

I'm your rainy day girl
Our two worlds collided with each other
Hand in hand in the sun
Two hearts became one
Loving each other
Best friends and best lovers

You're not alone
You have a love of your own
Someone to hold you when you're feeling lonely
I will always be near
No need to fear, I'll be with you forever
All your tears will disappear
And we'll be
Together
Forever

Now I walk in the rain by your side
There are no more tears for the rain to hide
Sunny days are abound
True love's what we found
Love is all around us

I'm so glad
I'm your rainy day girl
True love's what we found
Love is all around us

It makes me happy to be
Your rainy day girl

SHE'S A COUNTRY LADY

She lives in the city
That's not where she wants to be
She looks so pretty
She wants to trade her suit for blue jeans

She's tired of city life
There's too much strife
She wants to slow down
She's got to get out of town

She's a country lady
She has dreams of leaving the big city
Something has to change
She needs to find a way
Deep in her heart she knows
She's a country lady

She's always wanted
A place where she can make an escape
She's always needed
To feel a soft and sweet country breeze

She wants to walk around with bare feet on the ground
She needs to slow down
She's got to get out of town

She's a country lady
She has dreams of leaving the big city

Something has to change
She needs to find a way
Deep in her heart she knows
She's a country lady

She's lived in the city all of her life
She hasn't seen the stars on a clear warm night
She's only seen the city lights and dreaming of country nights

She works in the city
That's not where she wants to be
She's a southern beauty
Making plans for her getaway

She's tired of city life
There's too much strife
She wants to slow down
She's got to get out of town

She's a country lady
She has dreams of leaving the big city
Something has to change
She needs to find a way
Deep in her heart she knows
She's a country lady

I DREAMED I WAS YOU

I fell asleep for a very long time
When I woke I thought it was still today
Years had passed like a lightening flash
Time kept ticking away

Many people ask me what I did in my long sleep
I tell them I dreamed
They usually ask, "What did you dream about?"
I answer, "I dreamed I was you."

I dreamed I was all living things
I dreamed I was a seed
I thirsted
And when I drank
I burst forth from the seeds shell into the world of life
Freeing myself from containment of darkness

I reached for the sun and grew into a tree
The largest, tallest, most beautiful tree ever seen
My branches stretched forth throughout the lands
And I breathed life into all the inhabitants thereof
From my mouth I did kiss all living kind with my love

Forever we dwelled together
Never could we part
We were each other
We shared the same heart

Our hearts are made of liquid love
A forever flowing river without time
No obstacles to overcome
No mountains to climb

I could see my reflection in the water
My branches stretched far as the eye could see
In the reflection I saw every living thing
For the first time, I saw me

It began to rain
Tears covered all the land
Cooling the inner core
Protecting and starting again
All hearts trembled
All voices silenced
Contemplating the choices
Making ultimate sacrifices

Then a new day came
A day brighter than the sun
Shining down upon me
And the hearts of everyone
A new world began
And it was good
Love swept through the lands
I understood

There were no empty spaces
No sense of time
No rules to follow
No living thing blind

Eternal embracing
Back to one
Living in paradise
A new life had begun

This is what I dreamed
When I dreamed I was you

THE BRAVE

I live and I breathe in the land of the brave
Proud of my country in so many ways
The air is so sweet
The grass is so green
The most beautiful place that I've ever seen

It's where dreams come true if you want them to
There's no end to what you can do
Oh how I love the USA

America, America
Land of hope and the free
America, America
God bless the home of the brave

This land is built on love, trust and faith
We open our arms to all religions and race
No turning our backs on people in need
We help everyone that wants to live free

We lend our hand to every country in the world
To keep freedom and peace for every boy and girl
Oh how I love the USA

America, America
Land of hope and the free
America, America
God bless the home of the brave

We dream of peace for the world
But we can't do it on our own
We need everyone to help us reach that goal
Remember our children they need us so

America
Home of the free
Where our forefathers fought for our liberty
They lived and died for you and me
God bless the home of the brave
God bless the home of the brave

BACK TO BACK

Here comes the night
Another sleepless night
I'm so tired of fighting
Tired of hiding

Neither one of us wants to be the first to say I'm sorry
Back to back we lay

The night seems so long
When no one admits their wrong
And you can't close your eyes

Silence fills the room
The quiet sets the mood
Two hearts are aching

Here comes the night
Another sleepless night
Two hearts gone astray
We'll try to find our way
In a new days light

Neither one of us wants to be the first
To carry the weight
Or say any words
Neither one of us
Has the courage to say I'm sorry
Back to back we lay

No dreaming tonight
On this sleepless night
We're both tired of fighting
Tired of lying

Thinking about the day
And what you're going to say
But you won't say goodnight

Two hearts turn away
Blue skies turn to grey
Here comes the moonlight

Here comes the night
Another sleepless night
Two hearts on the mend
Try starting again
In a new days light

Neither one of us wants to be the first
To break the ice
Or speak any words
Neither one of us can sleep tonight
We'll both be awake
'Till the morning light

Holding back tears
Both hurting inside
We're both tired of fighting
Tired of trying

We both face the wall

No relief in sight at all
Two hearts are breaking

Here comes the night
Another sleepless night
Two hearts gone astray
We'll try to find our way
In a new days light

Neither one of us wants to be the first
To carry the weight
Or say any words
Neither one of us
Has the courage to say I'm sorry
Back to back we lay

Our eyes open wide
Back to back
Trying our best to hide

No hope in sight
It's going to be a sleepless night

Two lives gone astray
Will we move on and forget today?

Back to back we lay
Each facing our own way
Two hearts are frozen
Our love is broken

Here comes the night

Another sleepless night
I'm so tired of fighting
Tired of hiding

Neither one of us wants to be the first to say I'm sorry
Back to back we lay

Neither one of us has the courage to say I love you

BROKEN PROMISES

You promised me a better life
You said everything would be alright
All we seem to do is fight
Nothing has worked out right
I can't go on living this way
I have a future no matter what you say

I'm not going to fall with you to the ground
I'm going to stand tall no one can bring me down
You broke every promise
You broke my heart
Our love was a game
You won from the start

I always had faith that you'd change
Now I can see there's just no way
My faith has gone away

All you ever gave me were broken promises
I thought you really loved me
How wrong I was
We've wasted so much time
I thought I was yours
I thought you were mine
But I don't need your broken promises

Our world fell apart with all your secrecy
There's no way back to what we use to be

You broke every promise
You tore us apart
You killed every dream
You shot me in the dark

I know that you'll never change
You'll always be exactly the same
That's why I have to walk away

All you ever gave me were broken promises
I thought you really loved me
How wrong I was
We wasted so much time
I thought I was yours
I thought you were mine
But I don't need your broken promises

I'd never do what you did to me
I'd never make a promise that I couldn't keep
It seems you live a life full of lies
You hurt me so deep inside

What happened to you?
What made you this way?
Why did you tell me things you didn't mean to say?
Why did you lie?
What did you think you would gain?
I dried my eyes
I broke free from your chains

It's you that needs to learn how to change
But we both know there's just no way

My life is starting over today

All you ever gave me were broken promises
I thought you really loved me
How wrong I was
We wasted so much time
I thought I was yours
I thought you were mine
But I don't need your broken promises
No more broken promises

NOTHING LASTS

There's something about you that I can't explain
My hearts doing flips driving me insane
The days go by
I'm wasting time
I want to make you mine

Soon you'll be in someone else's arms
Sharing your love and giving all of your charm
It wouldn't have to be this way
If I only had the words to say

How will I ever know?
How will I ever see?
If I keep my dreams locked deep inside
My mind will never be free

Nothing seems to last forever
The sooner the better it's now or never
I don't know how long I'll wait
If I wait too long it may be too late

Every day I want to tell you I love you
Something inside me makes me scared as hell
I don't know when I'll get the courage
I guess only time will tell

The days go by
I'm still wasting time

I should say what's on my mind

How will I ever know?
How will I ever see?
If I keep my dreams locked deep inside
My mind will never be free

Nothing seems to last forever
The sooner the better it's now or never
I don't know how long I'll wait
If I wait too long it may be too late

21 LOVERS LANE

I wish that Cancer was just an astrological sign
The disease that shares the same name
Took the girl that was mine

She was young and full of fun
Her life had just begun
She had a smile that was bright
Eyes that shined in the night
She liked everyone

She had a heart full of love
She loved God above
I loved her and she loved me
Her favorite place was Sunset Beach
At 21 Lovers Lane

We use to walk all the way to 21 Lovers Lane
Watching the ocean
Drinking champagne
Dancing to the band
Walk the beach hand in hand
Watching the sun fade away
Just me and my girl
In our corner of the world
At 21 Lovers Lane

That's the way that it was
We shared each other's love

It seems like yesterday
I miss the look in your eyes
Staring at the skies
Wondering what tomorrow would bring

Then one day tomorrow never came
Time stopped at 21 Lovers Lane
The Sun forgot to rise
Clouds filled the skies
Down came the rain

Smiles turned to tears
Happy memories erased the fears
That day I lost a friend
I thought of where it all began
At 21 Lovers Lane

We use to walk all the way
To 21 Lovers Lane
Watching the ocean
Drinking champagne
Dancing to the band
Walk the beach hand in hand
Watching the sun fade away
Just me and my girl
In our corner of the world
At 21 Lovers Lane

LETTING GO OF LOVE

I heard you found someone new
That you can tell all of your lies to
I feel bad for him
He's in the same situation you put me in

What will it take for you to see the mistakes you've been
making?
If you're doing to him what you did to me
I know his heart is breaking

You were easy to love
'Till I knew what you were made of
There's no easy way
No good words to say
When love starts slipping away

Losing a friend
Starting over again
Sometimes we learn the hard way
It's fun to fall in love
But letting go of love isn't easy

It's hard on your mind
It's hard on your heart
When the one you love says they want to part
We live and we learn
Sometimes love can't return
And we both have to go our own way

It feels so good to fall in love
But letting go of love isn't easy

You helped me see what I needed for me
No more hanging on
I was hanging too long
Our dreams started fading away
Time passed us by
We didn't see eye to eye
But we both saw our love drift away

There was no going back
To what we use to have
The past was done and so were we
It was fun to fall in love
But letting go of love isn't easy

It's hard on your mind
It's hard on your heart
When the one you love says they want to part
We live and we learn
Sometimes love can't return
And we both have to go our own way
It feels so good to fall in love
But letting go of love isn't easy
Letting go of love isn't easy

SOMETIMES YOU WIN, SOMETIMES YOU LOSE

Sometimes you win
Sometimes you lose
Sometimes you smile
Sometimes you get the blues

Sometimes you win
Sometimes you lose
In each and everything you do
There's a choice that you have to make
Don't give up no matter what it takes

You can stay on that road
But where will it lead?
A new direction may be what you need

You can sit at the crossroads wondering which way to turn
Where will you go?
What will you learn?

No matter which road you choose
Sometimes you win
Sometimes you lose

If you give up who knows what could have been
Reach for the top
Don't ever give in

Sometimes a dream can seem hard to reach
Dreams can come true
If you just believe

Whichever road you choose
Sometimes you win
Sometimes you lose

Always reach for the stars
Always follow your heart
Do it for you
Do what you've got to do
Make your wish come true

Everything will be just fine
Sometimes it takes a little more time
Sometimes you win
Sometimes you lose
Sometimes you smile
Sometimes you get the blues

IT'S BEEN A GOOD LIFE

I took a trip around the world
I met a beautiful girl
She stepped right out of my dreams
She is all I need

She said I love you
When we were sitting on her front porch swing
I reached into my pocket
And pulled out an engagement ring

Please be my wife
I said to her on one knee
I was shaking when she said yes
It was love in the first degree

We have traveled all around the world
We gave life to a boy and a girl
We watched them grow
We watched ourselves grow old
It's been a good life

I'm glad I took the time
To see the forest for the trees
To learn what's precious to me
You are all I need

Hey pretty lady
Come on and dance with me

Let's steal the night away
Under the stars just you and me

Times have changed and so have we
But nothing changed our love
We were right from the very start
It's you I've always dreamed of

We sit and talk of old times
We share our memories
Our youth comes back in our minds
We can make the clock unwind

My sweet lady
Take my hand and follow me
Let's run like when we were young
Running wild and so carefree

I'm so happy
I see the forest for the trees
Our love will stand the test of time
Forever it's you and me

Put your loving arms around me
I'll hold you tenderly
Just like we were young
Sitting on your front porch swing

I know what love is
Love, is loving you
That's all I ever wanted
It's been a good life loving you

NEXT TIME YOU'RE LONELY

Are you nervous?
Are you scared?
Did you think I wouldn't care?
I've been waiting right here for you all the while

In the daytime
In the night
I'll be there when things aren't right
I'll give comfort to you
I'll try to make you smile

I've had those feelings
The same as you
You're not alone
Sometimes I'm lonely like you

Next time you're lonely
I'll help you through your day
I'm only a phone call away
Next time you need me
I'll do anything for you
So you won't have to be so lonely

I would take you away to a secret place
I'd spend the day with you
And if by the night
There's still loneliness in sight
I'd stay right there with you

Because I'm lonely too

When you're feeling down and blue
Remember I might feel that way too
I know you'd do the same for me
As I would for you

Don't be nervous
Don't be scared
Now you know I've always cared
You don't have to be alone
I'll always be there

I comprehend what you've been through
You're not alone
Sometimes I'm lonely like you

Next time you're lonely
You don't have to hide
I'll be right by your side
Next time you need me
Don't run away
You can always count on me
Next time you're lonely

WATCHING THE WAGON WHEEL ROLL 'ROUND

When I was only 10 years old my Papa came to me
He said, "Son, you need to pack your things, it's time to move our family.
We're going to California
We're going to find our destiny
You and Becky get in the wagon, wait for Ma and me."

I packed my bag
I climbed inside
Becky sat there scared
Mama climbed inside with a bible in her hand
It was time to leave
We went ridin' across the land
I remember,

Watching the wagon wheel roll 'round
Taking us to another town
Down the long and winding trail
Over the mountains, through the trees
Wheels rolling through the valley streams
I wondered if I'd grow to be a man
Travlin' and livin' across the land

My little sister Becky, she died along the way
She caught the typhoid fever and God took her away
Papa led the way and Mama cried for days

As we traveled on, I watched her tombstone fade away

We got to California after months of riding hard
Mama was so weary and Papa was so tired
We made our destination
Ma and Pa and me
And I knew my sister Becky was watching over me

Somehow through the years, I grew to be a man
Travlin' and livin' across this land
I remember,

Watching the wagon wheel roll 'round
Taking us to another town
Down the long and winding trail
Over the mountains, through the trees
Wheels rolling through the valley streams
I wondered if I'd grow to be a man
Travlin' and livin' across the land

Now the years have passed, it seems I went from 10 to 93
I'm the last survivor to remember my family
And I'll always thank the Lord
For all he's done for me
And I know Ma and Pa and Becky
Are in heaven, waiting there for me

ROSES, RAINBOWS AND YOU

Long ago we planted a garden full of roses
Each one brings back memories of you
Today I saw a rainbow above our garden
And I chased it the way we used to do

I felt just like I did back then
You and me running in the wind
Never reaching the rainbows end
All the gold we needed was in our love

We loved blue skies
We loved the rain
We watched our roses through the windowpane
The garden still looks the same
The only thing missing is you

I love to watch the roses grow
Waiting for the next rainbow
Try to catch it before it goes away

Touch the colors
Smell the air
The scent from roses fills the air
Pretty colors everywhere
All that's missing is you

We planted white roses along the pathway
It almost felt like walking through a cloud

You looked like an angel in our garden
With beautiful roses all around

I'd watch you sit on your favorite bench
Think in the rain until your dress was drenched
The only thing between you and the sun
Were the clouds and the raindrops

We loved blue skies
We loved the rain
We watched our roses through the windowpane
The garden still looks the same
The only thing missing is you

I love to watch the roses grow
Waiting for the next rainbow
Try to catch it before it goes away

Touch the colors
Smell the air
The scent from roses fills the air
Pretty colors everywhere
All that's missing is you

Each year I watch our roses grow
And I learned long ago
There are three things that I love so
Our roses, rainbows and you

LOOKING AT THE OUTSIDE

You're always looking at the outside
Never looking at the inside
How will you ever know if you're really in love?

If someone's going to love you and show they care
Don't run away
Don't be scared
Give them a chance to say how they really feel

You never let your love light show
You're all alone again
You're afraid they'll always let you go
You're on your own again
You never look within

You haven't learned your lesson yet
What you see isn't always what you get
You can't judge just by the cover
That's not the way to love her
You've got to see under the skin
Stop looking on the outside
Try looking at the inside
That's when you'll really know
You found your true love

You have to take the time to learn who she is
Be more than her lover
Be her best friend

Put on the brakes and do whatever it takes

Show her that she's more than a passing fling
A girl you can love
Make her heart sing
Let her know you mean what you really feel

You never let your love light show
You're all alone again
You're afraid they'll always let you go
You're on your own again
You never look within

You haven't learned your lesson yet
What you see isn't always what you get
You can't judge just by the cover
That's not the way to love her
You've got to see under the skin
Stop looking on the outside
Try looking at the inside
That's when you'll really know
You found your true love

Stop looking at the outside
Try looking at the inside
That's when you will know you're really in love

HOLLY

Let me paint a picture for you
Of the prettiest girl I ever knew
She had bright blue eyes and long blonde hair
She looked like a dream I dreamed somewhere
I look for you but you're nowhere

Holly won't you come back home
Please don't leave me all alone
Holly won't you come back home
I don't want to dream alone
Holly, please come home

I woke one day and you weren't there
Just your make-up on the dresser
And an empty chair
No reflection in the mirror
Nights are lonely without you near
I wish you were here

Holly won't you come back home
Please don't leave me all alone
Holly won't you come back home
I don't want to dream alone
Holly, please come home

Love can sometimes make us blind
Two hearts that once shined
Are now lost in time

Somehow we'll both find our way
Won't you come back to me and stay

Holly won't you come back home
Please don't leave me all alone
Holly won't you come back home
Don't leave me dreaming all alone
Holly, please come home

TIME PLAYS THE GAME

Time plays the game
Until it's over
Watching it slip away
Until it's gone

If I had my way
I'd change it to be any time I wanted
Time and time again how I've wondered

Time has always had its way
With comedy and tragedy
Taking things away from me
A memory lost in time

New life replaces all the death
Time erases all regrets
Time brings the sunshine and time brings the rain

The people cannot see it
But deep inside they feel it
Time runs in your heart and it travels through your veins

Reflections change throughout the years
Broken dreams and shattered mirrors
Pieces of your life appear scattered across the floor

The past cannot be found again
It lives in memories deep within

Time eats the days away and it swallows all the nights

While searching for your peace of mind
You know your time will come to die
Time leaves it all behind
It will close and lock the door

Standing at the wishing well
I heard the sacred tower bells
Ringing through the valley
Echoing across the plains

One life is all you get to live
Time has no beginning and it has no end
It will always see the sunshine and it will always bring the
rain

History has proven
Through the relics and the ruins
Nothing lasts forever
Its only time that wins the game

Time plays the game
Wishful thoughts that I have pondered
Time and time again how I've wondered

TRAPPED

You've got me suffocated
No room to breathe I really hate it
I'm sick of being trapped
I'm taking my life back for me

Did you think about me or was it only of yourself?
You tried to shut me out
You never even cared about me

You finally got me thinking
Its freedom I've been seeking
It doesn't matter what you say
Nothing can make me stay

I feel trapped
I'm going to fight back
I have to get out
No one can hold me back
I feel trapped
I have to escape
I'm movin' on
I'm getting out of this place
I'm taking off my mask
I'm taking my life back
I don't want to be trapped

I feel like I'm on an island
I'm all alone and isolated

Watching ships go by
Leaving me to die
Alone

My head is such a mess
I'm tearing down this fence
You can't stop me

You finally got me thinking
Its freedom I've been seeking
It doesn't matter what you say
Nothing can make me stay

I feel trapped
I'm going to fight back
I have to get out
No one can hold me back
I feel trapped
I have to escape
I'm movin' on
I'm getting out of this place
I'm taking off my mask
I'm taking my life back
I don't want to be trapped

No more suffocation
No more strangulation
I'm breaking free today
Get out of my way
You can't stop me

You finally got me thinking

Its freedom I've been seeking
It doesn't matter what you say
Nothing can make me stay

I feel trapped
I'm going to fight back
I have to get out
No one can hold me back
I feel trapped
I have to escape
I'm movin' on
I'm getting out of this place
I'm taking off my mask
I'm taking my life back
I don't want to be trapped

TURN MY LIFE AROUND

Why do you push me around?
You call me names and you knock me down
I was such a fool for loving you
I did the best that I could do
What about you?

You think you can control me
Let me tell you, you're so wrong
I'll live life the way I want to
It's too late to work things through
I'm not going to be like you

I live for life, love and freedom
I need something good to believe in
I know I'll find someone
That loves me for everything I've done
I'm not going to let you bring me down
I'll turn my life around

You could have tried a little harder
You shoved me off the edge
Drowned me in deep water
I'm still alive
I know how to survive

It's a shame I have to go
It hurts me more than you could know
I know as time goes by

I won't even think to cry
I'll do the best that I can do
What about you?

I live for life, love and freedom
I need something good to believe in
I know I'll find someone
That loves me for everything I've done
I'm not going to let you bring me down
I'll turn my life around

DELUSIONS

It's a crying shame
You never did the things you said
You lost everything
You had delusions in your head
Look where it's got you now
You never opened up
You live inside yourself
You're paying the price right now
You're going to self destruct
You know you will

Too bad you got lost
You didn't think about the cost
You never heard a word I said
Forgot your family and your friends
You always thought no one could tell
But you were only fooling, fooling yourself
What do you expect from me?
You're out of touch with reality

Your mind is filled with mass confusion
You wake up in the night to your inner illusions
Lost in seclusion, trapped inside your head

You never believed me
You have no trust
Your paranoid delusions have ruined us
You always turn your back when times get tough

You're only fooling yourself
You're out of touch

You'll end up alone
Walking the streets nowhere to go
Shaking from the cold
No one to love you anymore
How could you want to be that way?
I guess you made your choice
I tried to help you change
You never cared what I had to say

You never believed me
You have no trust
Your paranoid delusions have ruined us
You always turn your back when times get tough
You're only fooling yourself
You're out of touch

Your mind is filled with mass confusion
You wake up in the night to your inner illusions
Lost in seclusion, trapped inside your head

You never stop to smell the roses
All you think about are false delusions
Wake up and get those thoughts out of your head
You're only fooling yourself
You're out of touch

I'M FEELING DOWN

I sat down and wrote a poem
About how we laughed all night long
And the times I thought you loved me

I lie down and cry alone at night
I wonder if you'll see the light
Life is lonely without you

There are no words that can express
How my heart is left with emptiness
You promised me we'd never part
If you ever change your mind
I'll be here for you to find
Please take a chance and turn around
I'm feeling down

I see your reflection in the mirror
A part of you, lives with me here
Broken glass and shattered dreams
Cut me up and torture me

We used to love each other
Where did we go wrong?
You were always putting me down
Your words cut me to the bone
I'd rather be alone

I light a smoke and hang my head

I wonder if I'll see you again
Dreams of you are all I see
Let me end this misery

The only words that I can say
To tell you how I feel today
You broke your promise, you broke my heart
If you ever change your mind
I'll be here for you to find
Please take a chance and turn around
I'm feeling down

I'LL HAVE TO DREAM ALONE

It suddenly came to my mind
That the rivers washed away the time
I'm not getting any younger
But how I hunger

Sunshine escapes from my heart
Like the tides of the ocean we drift apart
Our love can be saved
Maybe I'll catch a wave

I cry in the rain to hide my pain
Teardrops fall driving me insane
How can I ever explain?

Dreams of you seem to fade and go
As time goes by how will I ever know?
All I wanted was for you to be my own
But for now I'll have to dream alone

We laughed together
We walked hand in hand
Our smiles turned to tears
I didn't understand
We changed in different ways
We let love slip away

You turned your back to me and walked away
I watched you go

I didn't want it this way
What could I say?
To make you want to stay

I count the days that you've been away
I wonder how long I'll have to feel this pain
How can I ever explain?

Dreams of you seem to fade and go
As time goes by how will I ever know?
All I wanted was for you to be my own
But for now I'll have to dream alone

Won't you tell me I'm wrong and you're coming home?
I don't want to spend my whole life alone
Help me from drowning in the rain

I wish I could go back to a place in time
When nothing mattered, just you and I
We were perfect lovers
We had each other

No matter where we go from here
I'll always remember you my dear
I'm not getting any younger
But how I hunger

Won't you tell me I'm wrong and you're coming home?
I don't want to spend my whole life alone
Help me from drowning in the rain

Dreams of you seem to fade and go

As time goes by how will I ever know?
All I wanted was for you to be my own
But for now I'll have to dream alone

THE DECISION

I see you've made up your mind
You left it all behind
You threw me away
But that's ok
I'm sure we'll both get by
I guess I was blind
I didn't see your pain
Behind your eyes you live in the pouring rain

You kept your feelings inside
You didn't have to run and hide
That's a hard way to live
I was always here
But you never tried

I don't understand why you left when I was sleeping
I couldn't tell because you hid all your feelings

Don't you think you made the wrong decision?
You never realized you get what you're giving
The whole world's not to blame
When you lost everything
You're the only one to blame

Every day I wake up alone
It's no longer a happy home
So much has changed
It's just not the same without you

So many times we tried
Too many times you lied
You didn't see what that did to me
You hid your eyes

I know this time I won't see you anymore
I hope you find what it is you're looking for

Don't you think you made the wrong decision?
You never realized
You get what you're giving
The whole world's not to blame
When you lost everything
You're the only one to blame
It was your decision

Life can seem so hard
I know because I've been there
You read me wrong
Because I'm the one that really cared

I wish you had said goodbye
I wish you had took the time
That was so cold
Now you'll never know
I never lied

I must have been blind
I never saw it coming
You lost all your pride
I thought that we had something

Don't you think you made the wrong decision?
You never realized
You get what you're giving
The whole world's not to blame
When you lost everything
You're the only one to blame
It was your decision

LOVE SHOULD COME EASY

I haven't cried
Since our love died
It's time to move on with both of our lives
It's simple to see
There's no more you and me

I took some time to clear my mind
You had me confused
I felt confined
Another glass of whiskey
Couldn't hide the truth

I'm not sure if we really loved
I guess we didn't know each other good enough
We didn't take the time
We both gave up
Love shouldn't be so tough
Love should come easy

What we had turned out to be
Like a forest without a tree
It's too late for what used to be
Loving shouldn't be so hard
Love should come easy

Our love lost its way
Cupid's arrow went astray
Our love faded day by day

We used to always say
Loving each other was easy

Something inside us changed
We lost that special touch
Our dreams fell apart
You threw a dart at my heart
We both went our separate ways

I'm not sure if we really loved
I guess we didn't know each other good enough
We didn't take the time
We both gave up
Love shouldn't be so tough
Love should come easy

How did we lose our love?
What were we thinking of?
Why did we let our life fall apart at the seams?
The dreams we concealed were not a love that is real
We could touch but we couldn't feel

People can't live on just being in love
It took parting for our eyes to see
We learned love can't return
When you both let love slip away
Love shouldn't be so tough
Love should come easy

A LETTER LEFT BEHIND

When I'm gone, someday someone will find
My very last poem in the letter I left behind
I didn't hide it
I wanted you to find it
That's why I left it right there
It was right where you looked
Seeing was all it took

Seeing, is believing
Can you believe without seeing?
Can it be true, these words contained inside the letter you
found today I left behind?

With each word that you read
Did you see me in your head?
Did you know I am always here?
Before you were through I became you and you within me
You became the writer
I became the reader
We walked a mile in each other's shoes
I believe in you and if you believe in me
Together we shall never lose

Do you feel better after reading my letter?
Knowing that which you now know?
"What do I know?"
You ask with wonder
Now feel your heart glow

That's me inside you
That's you inside me
Together we create what I call our love energy

Man or woman
Adult or child
I dwell within all hearts
Tame and wild
From humans to the animals
From insects to trees
From atoms and molecules
Through the Earth and seas
Into worlds unseen
Into your sleeping dream
Into the day
Into the night
Even the darkness exists from my light

I always knew you would be the one to find the last poem I
wrote in the letter I left behind
Look in the mirror
That's me looking at you
I'm glad you can see me
Just like I see you

SAN FRANCISCO DREAMS

I remember Janis like it was yesterday
Wearing her favorite shirt made of frill
Sitting with me on our favorite green bench
Atop of Hippy Hill

Her dreams were as beautiful
As the stars in the sky
On the green bench we would smoke
Just Janis and I

The sound of her laughter
Still echoes throughout my mind
When I close my eyes
I can make time unwind

I can still feel the wind
Blowing her hair across my face
And the way she sat there thinking
While looking up into space

We used to talk about the rings of Saturn, Venus and Mars
The man on the Moon
Dreaming under the stars

We wondered about aliens from afar
We wished together upon a shooting star
We shared with each other our favorite things
We talked about hope, peace, love and our dreams

She lived on Noe Street
I lived in my jeans
We both loved life
We had San Francisco dreams

All the empty spaces
In my heart she filled
When we sat on our favorite green bench
Atop of Hippy Hill

For a moment
The whole world stood still
Just Janis and I
Atop of Hippy Hill

Janis will always be 27
Though I have grown old
Our green bench is still there
So I've been told

I still see Janis now and then
When I close my eyes
We're atop of Hippy Hill again

Janis wearing her favorite shirt made of frill
Sitting with me on our favorite green bench
Atop of Hippy Hill

Hand in hand
Time will always stand still
For Janis and I
Atop of Hippy Hill

BILLY'S
FIRST BASEBALL GAME

Billy is so excited!
Today is a special day
Billy's dad is taking him to his first baseball game

On their way to the stadium
Billy and his dad stopped at the sporting store
They both bought new baseball gloves
Hoping to catch a foul ball

While driving to the stadium
Billy could see the ballpark come into view
Billy's dream of seeing his first baseball game
Is about to come true

Billy's excitement grows!
Today he gets to see his favorite baseball stars play
Eating peanuts and cracker jacks
Cheering for his favorite team

They arrived at the parking lot
Billy and his dad grabbed their new baseball gloves
They walked to the gates to buy tickets
Then Billy saw the big lighted sign above

There was Billy's favorite player
Swinging a bat in 3-D

It was the biggest TV screen Billy had ever seen

When Billy and his dad went through the turnstile
Billy's smile was wider than a mile
They bought hot dogs, drinks and ballpark snacks
Found their seats, the park was packed

Everyone cheered as the teams took the field
Billy felt like it was a dream but this time it was real
Billy and his dad stood with the crowd
Singing the National Anthem strong and loud

Ken Griffey Jr. was there to throw out the first pitch
The game started on time without a single glitch
The organ started playing and Billy clapped along
"Take Me Out to the Ballgame" is Billy's favorite song

The pitcher warmed up as he stood on the mound
The crowd began to foot stomp shaking the ground
Billy's favorite player was first at bat
He swung so hard he lost his hat

POP!
Went the ball way up high
500 feet through the stadium sky
A homerun on the very first swing!
Billy love's this baseball game

It's the bottom of the 9th inning
The score is tied
Billy's favorite player steps up to the plate to give it one more
try

The pitcher winds up...
He throws a fastball
Billy's favorite player gives it his all
He takes the swing hard as he can
And out of the park went that ball for a homerun again

Billy's favorite team wins the game!
He didn't catch a foul ball this time
He will have to try another day

It's time to go home now
Nine innings lasted long
Billy thanked his dad for taking him to the game
Then fell asleep in the car all the way home

They pulled into the driveway
Billy's dad carried him inside
He tucked Billy in bed
And put his baseball glove by his side

In the pocket of the glove
Billy's dad put a surprise inside
Two tickets to Billy's second baseball game
Next Saturday night

Now Billy lies dreaming
As little boys will
Maybe dreaming of being a baseball pitcher
Throwing each ball with precision and skill
Striking out every batter
Celebrating a perfect game
Becoming a baseball legend

Being inducted into the Hall of Fame

When Billy wakes
He will be so excited
As he discovers the two tickets in his glove that his dad hid
inside it
Now Billy knows hopes, dreams and wishes can be achieved
All you have to do is simply believe

BARE BONES

Americans give away money to the needless
Leaving the poor with no home
Stripping me of my existence
All I have left is bare bones

I never asked for a handout
Just a helping hand up
Why do the rich turn away when a poor man is down on his
luck?

I once had a life too
Though it wasn't like the rich
I tried to help other people
Now I'm left to die in a ditch

I'm a "has been" and a "was been"
A man who lost his pride
Shunned away by the 21st Century society
They only wish me to die

Soon they will get their wish
Wishes always come true for the rich
And I guess it's true what they say
You have to live to die another day

So the beat goes on
Like Sonny and Cher once said
And the beat still continues

Though Sonny is now dead

So right he was
When he wrote that song
Long after him, me and you
The beat will go on

The rich will continue to turn their heads
Pretending not to see you
Wishing you were dead

The poor will keep on dreaming
Making wishes that will never come true
Never driving a Cadillac or Lamborghini
Never knowing what it's like to be you

I'm not the first or last to be poor
I'll never have a love of my own
I'm not a lucky one
I'm a man with bare bones

THE WIDOWED WIFE

Your life was taken for reasons unknown
You said you would be right back
You never came home
Now I'm a widowed wife
Standing alone
Lost in a crowd
Wandering around
Uncertain of which direction to go

Time passes by
So people say
Maybe love will find me again someday
Broken dreams can be sewn back together
Stitch by stitch life slowly get's better

Though a scar will remain as a reminder of the pain
I will cherish each day we shared
I'll get on with my life
Though now I'm a widowed wife
Whose heart is on the mend

I can't change the past
I've learned good things never last
Though they can always begin again

TUNNEL RUNNER

Living in the darkness
Hiding from your fears
A never ending tunnel of torture
You've been running for years

You fall asleep and dream
In that dream you fall asleep again
That dream becomes another dream
Your dream never ends

You're running in an unknown dimension
Existing with no beginning and no end
Stuck in the middle of nowhere
You are your only friend

Transparent walls confine you
You can feel but you cannot see
You're a tunnel runner on a never ending journey
Searching for a sense of reality

Have you got any farther from where you started?
Have you gone anywhere at all?
Are you running fast as lightening?
Or is it just a slow crawl?

Where are you trying to get to?
What if you're already there?
What if you ran so fast you passed yourself?

What if you looked back and saw nothing there?

What if you're in a coma?
Lying in a hospital bed
Hooked up to man's machines
Living alone inside your head

Detached from one world
Caught in an never ending swirl
Running through the tunnel of time
Collecting the pieces of your mind

You keep a diary no one can find
Remembering a moment in time
A moment that was more beautiful
Than words could ever say

It was the day you first saw the sun rise
The heat of the sun kissed your skin
You absorbed its beauty
You became one within

You open your eyes
The memory ends
You go back into the darkness
Starting over again

Another tunnel
An eternal day
Are you running to somewhere?
Or running away?

I HAVE HAD IT ALL

Once I had feelings
Once I had cares
Once I had love
I watched it all disappear

Once I knew you
Once I held you
Now you're a stranger
I don't even know you

Once I could look into your eyes
Once I could hear your voice
Now all I know is silence
You left me no choice

I know what I was
I know what I am
I have laughed and cried
I have won and lost
I have felt like a King
I have had it all
Now I have nothing

ANOTHER LOST SOUL

Feelings of anger, worries and fears
Unsure of direction
Holding back tears
Silently walking the streets of unknown
Leading me into darkness
No friends
No home

Frets and frowns
I'm nowhere bound
Where will I go?
I don't even know
I'll just wander around in this sleepy little town
I'm just another lost soul

ILLUSIONS WITHIN

In my deepest days of despair
I did not see you standing there
For my eyes could not yet see
In the truth of my mind
My thoughts are intertwined
With illusions and what is real

I search this empty space
Hoping to replace all I seem to have lost
What price must I pay to live again today?
To live is worth any cost

All I have to do is wish it to be so
What I wish for shall appear
Will it be real the things I see and feel?
Or illusions created within?

INFLICTION

I am still here
I don't know how I've done it
I don't even know why
Perhaps living is my punishment for the sins I have inflicted
on this earth

My body aches
I am so tired
Physically and mentally drained
I have endured years of inner conflict
Always fighting within myself

I am my own worst enemy
I am the hunter
I am the snare trap
I am the biting teeth that won't let go

There's no escape
Nowhere to hide
I am a victim of myself

THE END IS CLOSER THAN THE BEGINNING

As old age creeps into your life
The end becomes closer than you ever realized

If wishes came true
Would you start over again?
Would you make the same mistakes?
Would you have the same friends?
Maybe everything would change
Perhaps all would remain the same
Would you risk all you have learned?
Would you fulfill unanswered dreams?

How close is the end?
How far is the beginning?
Will you die tomorrow?
How long will you continue living?

Will it really matter what you leave behind?
You're material possessions?
You're peace of mind?

In one hundred years
Will anyone care what you've done?
In a thousand years
Will there still be a sun?

I AM JUST A MAN

You would never believe who I am
You would never believe what I have done
Though many years have passed between us
I'm still living under the sun
I'm not a god
I'm just a man
Why couldn't you ever see?
You forced me to die and live a life of lies
But at least I've lived free

However great the costs may be
I did what I had to do
I'll never go back to what I used to be
Would you?
I gave you everything I had
I gave my all to the world
I lost everything I ever loved
I even lost my little girl

I'm not immortal
I'm a human being
That's all I ever wanted to be
The world kept me trapped inside myself
I had to escape a life of misery
I gave up on the music
I left it all behind
If I had stayed where I was
I truly would have lost my mind

This is the way it is
It's the way things have to be
I'm never coming back for anyone
I don't owe you anything
So let me live my life
The way I chose it to be
What once was is now in the past
And will forever remain as history

With all that said
What's done is done
I just wanted to be free
Not having to hide and run
With these words to everyone
I can only hope you understand
I am no longer Elvis Presley
I am just a man

34 YEARS GONE

Time never stops
Time continues on
In the blink of an eye
Your 34 years gone

Every dream you ever dreamed
Froze you forever in your mind
Stopping the clock of life
Trying to run from time

Watching through the window
Reflections in the mirror
Your eyes tell the story
Time is always here

It seems like yesterday we were laughing
Singing and carrying on
I can hear you right here with me now
How can you be 34 years gone?

OPEN WOUNDS

They say time heals all wounds
I don't believe that's true
No matter how I've tried
I've never gotten over you
I look over my shoulder
It's the same old thing
You're never standing there
Just your picture in a frame

There will be another day to sleep
Another day to wake
Another day of hurt
Another day of heartache

Sad days will soon be behind me
Though closely they will follow
I'll keep living for today and hoping for tomorrow
I can't pretend the pain has began to subdue
I don't yet have the scars
I still have open wounds

FOREVER FRIENDS

From the first time our eyes met
I knew she was the girl for me
At first glance I felt her strength and honesty
From her first words I felt her sincerity

Her hair pulled back, beautifully braided
Showing every detail of her face
I knew at that very moment
I found the friend and true love I'd been waiting to embrace

From the first touch of her skin I could feel the warmth of
her heart
All my life I've waited it seems
There you were out of nowhere
Fulfilling each of my dreams

Many times in our lives we weep
Acquaintances may come and go
But true, loyal friends like us last forever
And best friends never let go

CAN YOU FEEL ME?

When the sun rises in the morning
You will know I am smiling upon you

When you walk through the sand
The warmth you feel beneath you is the warmth from my
heart

With each wave that touches your feet
You will feel the kisses I am sending you

When the wind blows softly, against your skin
It will be from each breath I have taken

When the ocean mist touches your beautiful face
You will feel the tears I have cried

When the sun settles in the evening
You will know I am always with you

PRECIOUS LIFE

I look at you with lonely eyes
Trying to find my way
Looking for answers to questions of the unknown

My body bleeds inside from a mind full of wonder and
confusion
The path I seem to follow is the path of destruction and great
loss which I always knew lied ahead of me

Could it be true that God giveth and God taketh away?
Or do we stand with many paths before us faced with choices
of direction created within ourselves?

Sometimes we take living for granted and forget what is
precious in life to us
What I have found to be precious in my journey in this life is
life itself

REACHING OUT

I wake up every morning
Praying my life was just a dream
Then I blink my eyes a few times
To see if this is reality
I look around at this strange place
And then I know it's real
But I don't want it to be

So I think of the time when I had nothing
And try to start my life again from there
No family
No friends
No memories
No fears

Starting over with life is almost unbearable
I can't imagine continuing this life alone
Somehow people do, and I hope I find the strength
For it would be a shame to waste all I have been blessed with
And for no one to remember my name

So I'll keep searching for answers
Hoping that someday
I'll find who I am
But until I do
I'll just be a lonely man

SILENT SCREAMS

Behind the wall of silence
All I can hear is the sound of my own screams
My heart has absorbed its last drop of moisture
Turning my heart into desert
Barren and dry
Thirsting for new life

I cry out hoping someone will hear
Helping me break down the walls that separate our worlds
No one comes
No one answers my cries
My screams return to me in echoes
Pounding in my brain
Stripping me of all existence
In a world of silent screams

With my back against the wall
To the floor I slowly fall
Stuck in a gridlock between realities
Am I here or there?
Am I anywhere?
Am I just a thought lost in time?

Maybe I am someone else's dream
Living in their world of silent screams
Existing only in their imagination
A broken crown of their creation
Becoming each other's reflection

Maybe it is I who sleeps
Maybe it is I who weeps
Could I have become my own dream?
Am I dreaming now?
Am I the dream itself?
Did I build this wall of silent screams?

Maybe it was you
Maybe I am you
Maybe it was me
Maybe you are me
Maybe you and I are both someone else's dream
Living in their world of silent screams

For as long as a mind is able to dream
I may never escape my silent screams
I'll sit on the floor
With my back against the wall
Hoping to wake up
Or to not wake at all

A DIFFERENT WAY

I can see in your eyes
Truth is always far away
Your deceptions and lies
Have made me turn a different way

What's true to you?
I haven't a clue
I didn't audition for your play
You played your part well
On a swirling carousel
Now our hearts have turned a different way

Even though I knew you were there
It's like David Copperfield made you vanish into thin air
Our love was tied to invisible wires
A relationship of smoke and mirrors
Can't survive through hidden tears
Like an old trick our dreams expired

Behind the scenes secrets are revealed
The truth is no longer concealed
The tricks aren't as much fun
When you know how they're done
We both live with love on the run

If we should ever meet again
Would you smile and say, "It's so nice to see to you!"
Or would you turn a different way?

Would you pretend we never met?
Climbing the stairs into your private jet
Flying way up high
Soaring through the sky on your California Holiday?

Trying to forget
No regret
Accepting it

All we can say
At the end of the day
Is we both went a different way

I WALK ON THORNS

Would you walk with me on a road of thorns?
Would you stay by my side?
Or would you leave me all alone
Bleeding
Dying

Would you look into my eyes?
Then turn and walk away?
Would you deny me?
With nothing to say

Would you walk with me on the road of thorns?
Or would you choose the road paved with gold?
Would you leave me desolate?
Tattered and torn
In complete solitude

Would you give a hand to a friend in need?
Or would you watch me suffer?
Letting me bleed

Would you offer me what I would offer you?
Would you have equal trust?
Would you release the good within you?
Or would you hide it until you're dust?

Would you walk with me on a road of thorns?
Would you stay by my side?

Helping each other live
Instead of helping each other die?

STARTING OVER

Before you can start anew
You have to let go of the past
Reach out your hand and grab the future
Hold it tight as you can
Without it there's no tomorrow
Can you let go of yesterday and all the days before?
Closing the door to the past forever more?
Put your car in drive
Step on the gas
Drive forward into the future
Never look back
Letting go of the past is not easy
It may be the hardest thing you'll ever do
Leave the night behind
Welcome the sunshine
Let your life start anew

THE COLORS OF MY WORLD

Dark blue waters
Bright blue skies
Green fields and butterflies
So many wonderful colors to see with my eyes!

The big yellow sun
White clouds in the air
Brown dirt of the earth
Bright lights at the fair
There are beautiful colors everywhere!

Pink carnations
Bumble bees
Red balloons and Christmas trees
Rainbows and ribbons
Changing of the leaves
There are so many wonderful colors to see!

Orange pumpkins and golden rings
Silver coins and shiny things
Purple horizons and bright moonbeams
These are the colors of my world

Birthday cakes and ice cream too
Made from colors of every hue
There's a color for everything in view
There are even colors you never knew

Take my hand
I'll show you too
There's a colorful world waiting for you!

WITH OPEN ARMS

Lord, when my final day shall come
Take my hand and show me life beyond the Sun
I'll be waiting to embrace all your love
With open arms

I'll see your precious land oh Lord
In ways I've never imagined before
Exploring a new world
Living inside your love

Your kindness completes my soul
Together we are whole
From the heart of the river we flow
Like a leaf on a stream

Riding a rainbow across the sky
On wings of an angel we fly
Absorbing beauty together
With open arms

We share the same heart and soul
Your love helps me to know
With knowledge I grow
Always loving you

I'll always praise your name
And remember from where I came
I thank you for all I know

With open arms

In my final moment of life
I'll see your glory and light
Then I shall come to you
With my arms open wide

Lift me up when it's my time
Shine your love on me so divine
And I know you'll be there waiting
With open arms

"Everyone needs something to believe in. If we stop believing we lose hope, fall into despair and become trapped within ourselves."

- Connor Tifarra November 7, 2007

"It seems many people require an answer to everything that brings wonder to the mind. In my deepest contemplation on a question that yields no absolute conclusion, I accept that it simply "IS" and question no further."

- Connor Tifarra January 3, 2010

CROSSING
A NARROW BRIDGE

Connor Tifarra Entertainment

www.ingramcontent.com/pod-product-compliance
Lightning Source LLC
Chambersburg PA
CBHW071004040426
42443CB00007B/658